# Forex Essentials:

# A Beginner's Guide to Trading Currencies

Chapters:

# Chapter 1: Introduction to Forex

Welcome to the world of Forex! The Foreign Exchange Market, or Forex, is a global market where individuals, businesses, and institutions trade currencies. It's a vast and exciting market, with a daily trading volume of over $6 trillion.

*What is Forex?*

The Foreign Exchange market, commonly referred to as Forex, is the largest and most liquid financial market in the world. It is a global decentralized market where individuals, businesses, and institutions trade currencies.

*Why trade Forex?*

1. Liquidity: Forex is the most liquid market in the world, with a vast number of participants and a high trading volume.

2. Market Accessibility: Trade from anywhere with an internet connection, 24 hours a day, 5 days a week.

3. Diversification: Add currency trading to your investment portfolio to reduce risk and increase potential returns.

4. Potential for High Returns: Leverage and market volatility can lead to significant gains (and losses).

*How does Forex work?*

Forex trading involves buying one currency while simultaneously selling another. The goal is to profit from the fluctuations in exchange rates. Forex trading can be done through various channels, including:

- Spot market: Immediate trading at current market prices

- Forward market: Trading at predetermined future prices

- Futures market: Trading contracts with standardized terms

Before you begin trading, it's essential to:

1. Educate yourself: Learn the basics of Forex trading and risk management.

2. Set clear goals: Define your trading objectives and risk tolerance.

3. Choose a broker: Select a reputable and reliable Forex broker.

## History of Forex

The Forex market has a rich history that dates back to ancient civilizations:

- Early Currency Trading: Currency trading originated in ancient Mesopotamia around 3000 BC.

- Gold Standard: The gold standard was introduced in the 19th century, where currencies were pegged to gold.

- Bretton Woods Agreement: In 1944, the Bretton Woods Agreement established a fixed exchange rate system, which collapsed in 1971.

- Floating Exchange Rates: The Forex market transitioned to floating exchange rates in the 1970s, allowing for modern Forex trading.

- Electronic Trading: The advent of electronic trading in the 1990s revolutionized Forex, making it more accessible and efficient.

## Key Events that Shaped Forex

- 1971: Nixon Shock: The US abandoned the gold standard, leading to floating exchange rates.

- 1990s: Emergence of Online Trading: Electronic trading platforms emerged, making Forex accessible to individual traders.

- 2008: Global Financial Crisis: The crisis highlighted the importance of Forex in global finance.

## Forex Market Participants

The Forex market is comprised of various participants, each playing a vital role:

1. Banks and Financial Institutions: Major players in Forex, accounting for the majority of trading volume.

2. Central Banks: Responsible for monetary policy, currency management, and intervention.

3. Hedge Funds and Institutional Investors: Manage large sums of money, often using Forex as a diversification tool.

4. Individual Retail Traders: Private traders, often using online trading platforms.

5. Corporations and Businesses: Engage in Forex for import/export purposes, hedging, and investment.

6. Market Makers and Brokers: Facilitate trading, providing liquidity and execution services.

7. Speculators and Day Traders: Focus on short-term profits, often using technical analysis.

*Forex Market Structure*

- Interbank Market: Banks and financial institutions trade among themselves.

- Over-the-Counter (OTC) Market: Decentralized market where participants trade directly.

- Exchange-Traded Market: Currencies traded on exchanges, like futures and options.

*Forex Market Size and Liquidity*

The Forex market is the largest and most liquid financial market globally:

- Daily Trading Volume: Exceeds $6 trillion, dwarfing other financial markets.

- Liquidity: High liquidity allows for seamless execution of trades.

- Market Hours: Forex market is open 24/5, Monday to Friday.

*Forex Market Benefits*

- Accessibility: Trade from anywhere with an internet connection.

- Leverage: Use margin to control large positions with a small amount of capital.

- Liquidity: Enter and exit trades quickly, even in large quantities.

- Market Volatility: Take advantage of price movements in both directions.

- Diversification: Trade a variety of currency pairs, reducing dependence on a single market.

*Forex Market Risks*

- Market Volatility: Prices can fluctuate rapidly, resulting in losses.

- Leverage: Amplifies both gains and losses.

- Liquidity Risks: Market conditions can change quickly, affecting trade execution.

- Counterparty Risks: Risk of default by the other party in a trade.

*Forex Market Hours and Sessions*

The Forex market operates 24 hours a day, 5 days a week. It's divided into three major trading sessions.

1. Asian Session (Tokyo, Sydney, Hong Kong): 23:00 - 08:00 GMT

2. European Session (London, Frankfurt, Paris): 07:00 - 16:00 GMT

3. North American Session (New York, Chicago, Toronto): 13:00 - 22:00 GMT

Market Overlaps

- Asian-European Overlap: 07:00 - 08:00 GMT

- European-North American Overlap: 13:00 - 16:00 GMT

Highest Liquidity

- European-North American Overlap: 13:00 - 16:00 GMT (best time to trade)

Market Closures

- Weekends: Forex market is closed

- Holidays: Market may be closed or have limited hours

# Chapter 2: Understanding Currency Pairs

*Currency Pair Basics*

In Forex, currencies are traded in pairs, with each pair representing the exchange rate between two currencies. Understanding currency pairs is crucial for successful Forex trading.

Major Currency Pairs

- EUR/USD (Euro vs. US Dollar)

- USD/JPY (US Dollar vs. Japanese Yen)

- GBP/USD (British Pound vs. US Dollar)

- USD/CHF (US Dollar vs. Swiss Franc)

- AUD/USD (Australian Dollar vs. US Dollar)

*Currency Pair Notation*

- Base Currency: The first currency in the pair (e.g., EUR in EUR/USD)

- Quote Currency: The second currency in the pair (e.g., USD in EUR/USD)

- Bid Price: The price at which you can sell the base currency

- Ask Price: The price at which you can buy the base currency

*Currency Pair Characteristics*

Each currency pair has unique characteristics that affect its behavior:

1. Volatility: Measure of price fluctuations (e.g., EUR/JPY is more volatile than EUR/USD)

2. Liquidity: Ease of entering/exiting trades (e.g., EUR/USD is more liquid than EUR/NOK)

3. Spread: Difference between bid/ask prices (e.g., EUR/USD has a tighter spread than EUR/TRY)

4. Trading Range: Historical price range (e.g., USD/JPY has a wider trading range than USD/CHF)

5. Correlation: Relationship between currency pairs (e.g., EUR/USD and GBP/USD are positively correlated)

6. Market Sentiment: Overall attitude towards a currency pair (e.g., bullish or bearish)

7. Economic Indicators: Influential economic data releases (e.g., GDP, inflation, interest rates)

Understanding these characteristics helps traders:

- Identify profitable trading opportunities

- Manage risk effectively

- Set realistic expectations

*Major Currency Pair Groups*

1. Majors: Most widely traded pairs, highly liquid, and tight spreads

- EUR/USD, USD/JPY, GBP/USD, USD/CHF, AUD/USD

2. Crosses: Pairs that don't include the US dollar, often less liquid

- EUR/JPY, EUR/GBP, AUD/NZD, CAD/JPY

3. Commodity Pairs: Currencies closely tied to commodity prices

- AUD/USD (gold), CAD/USD (oil), NZD/USD (dairy)

4. Emerging Market Pairs: Currencies from developing economies

- USD/TRY (Turkey), USD/ZAR (South Africa), USD/MXN (Mexico)

5. Exotic Pairs: Less commonly traded pairs, often with higher spreads

*Currency Pair Trading Strategies*

1. Trend Following: Suitable for majors and commodity pairs

- Ride long-term trends

- Use indicators like Moving Averages, MACD

2. Range Trading: Effective for crosses and emerging market pairs

- Identify support/resistance levels

- Use indicators like Bollinger Bands, Stochastic Oscillator

3. Scalping: Best for majors and highly liquid pairs

- Take advantage of small price movements

- Use indicators like RSI, Momentum

4. Carry Trading: Suitable for pairs with significant interest rate differences

- Hold positions for extended periods

- Earn interest rate differentials

5. Mean Reversion: Effective for pairs with high volatility

- Identify overbought/oversold conditions

- Use indicators like RSI, Bollinger Bands

Understanding these strategies helps traders:

- Develop effective trading plans

- Adapt to changing market conditions

- Manage risk and maximize profits

*Currency Pair Correlations*

Understanding correlations between currency pairs is crucial for:

1. Diversification: Spread risk across uncorrelated pairs

2. Hedging: Reduce exposure to market fluctuations

3. Trade management: Adjust positions based on correlation changes

Common correlations

1. Positive Correlation: Pairs move together (e.g., EUR/USD and GBP/USD)

2. Negative Correlation: Pairs move in opposite directions (e.g., EUR/USD and USD/CHF)

3. No Correlation: Pairs move independently (e.g., EUR/USD and AUD/JPY)

Correlation Coefficient:

- Measures correlation strength (-1 to 1)

- Helps identify potential trading opportunities

Monitoring Correlations:

- Use correlation tables or software

- Adjust trading strategies accordingly

# Chapter 3: Exchange Rates and Quotes

*Understanding Exchange Rates*

An exchange rate is the price of one currency in terms of another. It's a crucial concept in Forex trading.

Exchange Rate Types:

1. Spot Rate: Current market price

2. Forward Rate: Price for future delivery

3. Swap Rate: Difference between spot and forward rates

Exchange Rate Notation:

- Bid Price: Sell price (always lower)

- Ask Price: Buy price (always higher)

- Bid-Ask Spread: Difference between bid and ask prices

Exchange Rate Conventions:

- Direct Quote: Domestic currency per unit of foreign currency (e.g., USD/JPY)

- Indirect Quote: Foreign currency per unit of domestic currency (e.g., JPY/USD)


Quote Structure:

- Base Currency: First currency in the pair (e.g., EUR in EUR/USD)

- Quote Currency: Second currency in the pair (e.g., USD in EUR/USD)

- Bid Price: Sell price (e.g., 1.1000)

- Ask Price: Buy price (e.g., 1.1005)

Quote Examples:

- EUR/USD: 1.1000/1.1005 (bid/ask)

- USD/JPY: 110.50/110.70 (bid/ask)

Pip Value:

- Smallest unit of price movement (e.g., 0.0001 for EUR/USD)

- Used to calculate profits/losses

*Exchange Rate Calculations*

Conversion Calculations:

- Base Currency to Quote Currency: Multiply by ask price

- Quote Currency to Base Currency: Divide by bid price

Profit/Loss Calculations:

- _ Pip Value x Number of Pips = Profit/Loss_

- Profit/Loss x Lot Size = Total Profit/Loss

Example Calculations:

- EUR/USD: 1.1000/1.1005, buy 1 lot (100,000 EUR)

- Sell at 1.1010, profit = 5 pips x 100,000 EUR = $500


*Cross Rates and Triangulation*

Cross Rates:

- Exchange rate between two currencies not involving the base currency

- Calculated using two related major currency pairs

Example:

- EUR/JPY cross rate = (EUR/USD x USD/JPY)

Triangulation:

- Involves three currencies and two exchange rates

- Used to verify accuracy or find arbitrage opportunities

Example:

- EUR/USD, USD/JPY, and EUR/JPY form a triangulation

Arbitrage Opportunity:

- Buy EUR/JPY at 130.00, sell EUR/USD at 1.1000, and sell USD/JPY at 117.00

- Lock in risk-free profit (if exchange rates are inefficient)

*Exchange Rate Regimes*

Fixed Exchange Rate Regime:

- Currency pegged to a stronger currency or basket

- Central bank intervenes to maintain fixed rate

Floating Exchange Rate Regime:

- Currency value determined by market forces

- Central bank may intervene occasionally

Managed Float Regime:

- Hybrid of fixed and floating regimes

- Central bank influences exchange rate without fixing it

Pegged Exchange Rate Regime:

- Currency pegged to a stronger currency or basket

- Central bank allows limited fluctuations

Trading Implications:

- Fixed regimes: reduced volatility, predictable movements

- Floating regimes: increased volatility, market-driven movements

# Chapter 4: Market Participants and Structure

*Market Participants*

The Forex market comprises various participants, each with different goals and strategies:

1. Banks and Financial Institutions:

- Provide liquidity and facilitate transactions

- Trade for clients and their own accounts

2. Central Banks:

- Regulate and stabilize their domestic currencies

- Implement monetary policies

3. Investment Funds and Asset Managers:

- Manage portfolios and invest in currencies

- Seek returns through currency appreciation

4. Corporations and Multinationals:

- Engage in international trade and investment

- Hedge currency risk

5. Retail Traders and Individuals:

- Trade for speculation or hedging

- Utilize online platforms and brokers

*Market Structure*

1. Interbank Market:

- Top-tier banks and financial institutions trade among themselves

- Determines exchange rates and liquidity

2. Tier 1 and Tier 2 Banks:

- Smaller banks and financial institutions trade with top-tier banks

- Access to liquidity and competitive pricing

3. Brokers and Prime Brokers:

- Facilitate trades for clients and provide liquidity

- Offer competitive pricing and execution

4. Retail Market:

- Individual traders and small institutions trade through brokers

- Access to Forex market through online platforms


*Market Makers and Liquidity Providers*

Market Makers:

- Quote both buy and sell prices (bid/ask)

- Profit from bid-ask spread

- Provide liquidity and maintain market stability

Liquidity Providers:

- Supply liquidity to market makers and brokers

- Can be banks, hedge funds, or other financial institutions

- Earn fees or profits from providing liquidity

Characteristics:

- Market makers: quote stability, tight spreads, and high liquidity

- Liquidity providers: deep pockets, market expertise, and risk management

Trading Implications:

- Market makers' quotes can influence exchange rates

- Liquidity providers' actions can impact market volatility


*Electronic Communication Networks (ECNs) and Straight-Through Processing (STP)*

Electronic Communication Networks (ECNs):

- Electronic platforms connecting buyers and sellers directly

- No intermediaries, reducing costs and increasing transparency

- ECNs match trades and provide liquidity

Straight-Through Processing (STP):

- Automated processing of trades without human intervention

- Trades executed directly with liquidity providers

- Reduces errors, increases speed, and improves efficiency

Benefits:

- Improved liquidity and tighter spreads

- Increased transparency and reduced costs

- Faster execution and reduced slippage

Trading Implications:

- ECNs and STP enable more efficient and cost-effective trading

- Traders can access deeper liquidity pools and tighter spreads

# Chapter 5: Trading Sessions and Market Hours

*Understanding Trading Sessions*

The Forex market operates 24/5, divided into four major trading sessions:

1. Sydney Session (22:00 - 08:00 GMT):

- Australian and New Zealand markets open

- Liquidity increases, volatility rises

2. Tokyo Session (00:00 - 09:00 GMT):

- Japanese market opens

- Asian markets' influence grows

3. London Session (08:00 - 17:00 GMT):

- European markets open

- Highest liquidity and volatility

4. New York Session (14:00 - 22:00 GMT):

- US market opens

- American and European markets overlap

Understanding trading sessions helps traders:

- Identify optimal trading times

- Anticipate market movements

- Manage risk effectively


Overlapping Sessions:

- Increased liquidity and volatility

- Higher trading activity and market movements

- London-New York overlap (14:00-17:00 GMT): peak market hours


Market Hours:

- Weekdays: 22:00 GMT Sunday - 22:00 GMT Friday

- Weekends: market closed

- Holidays: reduced liquidity and volatility

Key Market Hours:

- 08:00 GMT: London session opens

- 14:00 GMT: New York session opens

- 17:00 GMT: London session closes

- 22:00 GMT: New York session closes

Understanding overlapping sessions and market hours helps traders:

- Plan trading strategies

- Manage risk and volatility

- Capitalize on market opportunities

*Time Zone Considerations and Market Open/Close Times*

Time zone considerations and market open/close times are crucial.

Time Zones:

- GMT (Greenwich Mean Time): standard Forex market time zone

- EST (Eastern Standard Time): New York session time zone

- CST (Central Standard Time): Chicago time zone

- PST (Pacific Standard Time): Los Angeles time zone

Market Open/Close Times:

- Sydney: 22:00 GMT (Sunday) - 08:00 GMT (Friday)

- Tokyo: 00:00 GMT (Monday) - 09:00 GMT (Friday)

- London: 08:00 GMT (Monday) - 17:00 GMT (Friday)

- New York: 14:00 GMT (Monday) - 22:00 GMT (Friday)

# Chapter 6: Forex Trading Platforms and Tools

*Overview of Forex Trading Platforms*

Proprietary Platforms:

- Developed by brokers for their clients

- Customized features and interfaces

- Examples: MetaTrader, cTrader, and NinjaTrader

Third-Party Platforms:

- Independent platforms offering advanced features

- Compatible with multiple brokers

- Examples: TradingView, Thinkorswim, and ZuluTrade

Web-Based Platforms:

- Accessible via web browsers

- No software download required

- Examples: MetaTrader WebTrader and cTrader Web

Mobile Platforms:

- Trading on-the-go via mobile devices

- Apps for iOS and Android devices

- Examples: MetaTrader Mobile and cTrader Mobile

*Key Features of Forex Trading Platforms*

Charting and Technical Analysis:

- Real-time charts and technical indicators

- Customizable charting packages

Order Management:

- Market, limit, stop, and trailing stop orders

- One-click trading and trade management

Risk Management:

- Stop-loss and take-profit orders

- Position sizing and margin management

Market Data and News:

- Real-time market data and news feeds

- Economic calendar and market analysis

Backtesting and Strategy Development:

- Historical data for backtesting strategies

- Strategy builders and automated trading

Customization and Integration:

- Customizable interfaces and workflows

- Integration with third-party tools and APIs

*Advanced Features and Tools*

Algorithmic Trading:

- Automated trading strategies using Expert Advisors (EAs)

- Customizable trading robots and scripts

VPS (Virtual Private Server) Hosting:

- Remote hosting for automated trading systems

- Reduced latency and increased uptime

Market Scanners and Alerts:

- Real-time market scanning and alerts

- Customizable criteria and notifications


Social Trading and Copy Trading:

- Follow and copy trades from experienced traders

- Social trading networks and communities


APIs and Custom Integration:

- Application Programming Interfaces (APIs) for custom integration

- Connect with third-party tools and platforms


These advanced features and tools can enhance trading performance and efficiency.

# Chapter 7: Order Types and Execution

*Understanding Order Types*

1. Market Order:

- Buy or sell at current market price

- Immediate execution

2. Limit Order:

- Buy or sell at specified price or better

- No guarantee of execution

3. Stop Order:

- Buy or sell when price reaches specified level

- Used for risk management or entries

4. Stop-Limit Order:

- Combination of stop and limit orders

- Specifies price range for execution


Understanding order types helps traders:

- Execute trades effectively

- Manage risk

- Achieve trading goals


*Advanced Order Types and Execution*

Advanced order types and execution options:

1. Take-Profit Order:

- Automatically closes trade when profit target reached

- Locks in profits

2. Trailing Stop Order:

- Moves stop-loss level as price moves in favor

- Maximizes profits

3. Breakout Order:

- Executes trade when price breaks through level

- Used for trend following

4. OCA (One Cancels All) Order:

- Group of orders; one execution cancels others

- Manages multiple trades

5. IFO (If-Then) Order:

- Conditional order; one action triggers another

- Automates trading strategies

*Execution options:*

1. Fill or Kill (FOK):

- Immediate execution or cancellation

2. Immediate or Cancel (IOC):

- Partial fill allowed; remainder canceled

3. Good Till Canceled (GTC):

- Order remains active until canceled

Understanding advanced order types and execution options helps traders:

- Implement complex trading strategies

- Manage risk and optimize profits

- Refine trading performance

*Slippage, Requotes, and Execution Risks*

1. Slippage:

- Difference between expected and actual execution price

- Caused by market volatility or liquidity issues

2. Requotes:

- Broker's request to confirm trade at current price

- May occur during high volatility or rapid price movement

3. Execution Risks:

- Failed or partial execution

- Price gaps or flash crashes

*Mitigating execution risks*

1. Choose a reliable broker:

- Look for brokers with good execution reputations

2. Use limit orders:

- Specify exact price for execution

3. Monitor market conditions:

- Avoid trading during high volatility or news events

4. Use risk management tools:

- Stop-loss and take-profit orders

Understanding execution risks and taking steps to mitigate them helps traders:

- Minimize losses

- Maximize profits

- Refine trading performance

# Chapter 8: Risk Management

*Understanding Risk Management*

Risk Management Definition:

- The process of identifying, assessing, and controlling potential losses

- Essential for long-term trading success


Key Risk Management Concepts:

1. Risk-Reward Ratio:

- Balancing potential losses and gains

2. Position Sizing:

- Managing trade size to limit exposure

3. Stop-Loss Orders:

- Automating loss limitation

4. Leverage:

- Understanding the double-edged sword of borrowing


Effective risk management helps traders:

- Protect capital

- Maximize returns

- Develop discipline and confidence


*Risk Management Strategies*

1. Position Sizing:

- Calculate optimal trade size based on account size and risk tolerance

- Use formulas or risk management tools

2. Stop-Loss Placement:

- Set stop-losses based on technical levels, volatility, or risk-reward ratio

- Avoid placing stops too close to entry points

3. Risk-Reward Ratio:

- Set realistic risk-reward ratios (e.g., 1:2 or 1:3)

- Adjust ratios based on market conditions and strategy

4. Diversification:

- Spread risk across different currency pairs, assets, or strategies

- Avoid over-exposure to single markets or trades

5. Hedging:

- Use hedging strategies to mitigate risk (e.g., forex options or correlated pairs)

Implementing these strategies helps traders:

- Limit losses

- Maximize gains

- Develop a disciplined trading approach

*Advanced Risk Management Techniques*

1. Expected Drawdown:

- Calculate potential drawdown based on historical data

- Prepare for worst-case scenarios

2. Value-at-Risk (VaR) Modeling:

- Estimate potential losses with statistical models

- Set risk limits and adjust strategies

3. Stress Testing:

- Simulate extreme market scenarios

- Evaluate strategy performance and adjust risk management

4. Maximum Daily Loss Limits:

- Set daily loss limits to prevent significant drawdowns

- Adjust limits based on market conditions

5. Regular Portfolio Rebalancing:

- Periodically review and adjust trade sizes and risk exposure

- Maintain optimal risk-reward balance

Mastering these advanced techniques helps traders:

- Refine risk management skills

- Optimize strategy performance

- Achieve long-term trading success

# Chapter 9: Technical Analysis and Charting

*Introduction to Technical Analysis*

Technical analysis: studying charts to predict future price movements

Key Principles:

1. Market Action Discounts Everything:

- Prices reflect all market information

2. Prices Move in Trends:

- Trends are the foundation of technical analysis

3. History Repeats Itself:

- Patterns and trends repeat over time


*Types of Charts*

1. Line Charts:

- Simple, closing price-based charts

2. Bar Charts:

- Open-high-low-close (OHLC) charts

3. Candlestick Charts:

- Visual representation of price action


*Chart Patterns and Trends*

1. Uptrend:

- Successive higher highs and higher lows

2. Downtrend:

- Successive lower highs and lower lows

3. Sideways Trend:

- Flat, ranging market

Understanding technical analysis and charting helps traders:

- Identify trends and patterns

- Make informed trading decisions

- Develop a competitive edge

*Chart Patterns*

1. Reversal Patterns:

- Head and Shoulders, Inverse Head and Shoulders

- Double Tops and Bottoms

2. Continuation Patterns:

- Triangles, Wedges, and Pennants

- Flags and Channels

3. Breakout and Fakeout Patterns:

- Identifying genuine breakouts and false signals

Recognizing chart patterns and trends helps traders:

- Anticipate price movements

- Set realistic trading goals

- Improve entry and exit timing

*Trend Indicators*

1. Moving Averages (MA):

- Simple, Exponential, and Weighted MA

2. Relative Strength Index (RSI):

- Measures overbought and oversold conditions

3. Bollinger Bands:

- Volatility-based trend indicator

*Momentum Indicators*

1. Stochastic Oscillator:

- Compares closing price to price range

2. MACD (Moving Average Convergence Divergence):

- Signal line and histogram

3. Ichimoku Cloud:

- Comprehensive trend and momentum indicator

*Oscillators*

1. Force Index:

- Measures energy and momentum

2. Commodity Channel Index (CCI):

- Identifies overbought and oversold conditions

3. Williams %R:

- Measures overbought and oversold conditions

Using technical indicators and oscillators helps traders:

- Confirm trading decisions

- Identify potential reversals

- Refine entry and exit points

*Advanced Technical Analysis Techniques*

Fibonacci Analysis:

1. Fibonacci Retracement:

- Identifies potential support and resistance levels

2. Fibonacci Extensions:

- Projects price targets

Elliott Wave Theory:

1. Wave Patterns:

- Identifies trend and countertrend waves

2. Wave Counts:

- Predicts price movements

Harmonic Patterns:

1. Gartley Pattern:

- Identifies potential reversals

2. Bat Pattern:

- Identifies potential continuations

*Advanced Charting Techniques*

1. Multiple Time Frame Analysis:

- Confirms trading decisions

2. Intermarket Analysis:

- Identifies relationships between markets

Mastering advanced technical analysis techniques helps traders:

- Refine trading strategies

- Improve market understanding

- Enhance trading performance

# Chapter 10: Fundamental Analysis and Market News

*Introduction to Fundamental Analysis*

Fundamental analysis: studying economic and financial factors to predict currency value

Key Principles:

1. GDP and Economic Growth:

- A country's economic performance impacts currency value

2. Inflation and Interest Rates:

- Central banks' decisions influence currency value

3. Trade Balance and Current Account:

- A country's trade position impacts currency demand

*Fundamental Analysis Tools*

1. Economic Indicators:

- GDP, inflation, unemployment, and more

2. Central Bank Actions:

- Interest rate decisions and monetary policy

3. Government Policies:

- Fiscal policy, trade agreements, and political events

Understanding fundamental analysis helps traders:

- Identify long-term market trends

- Make informed trading decisions

*Market News and Event-Driven Trading*

Impactful News Events:

1. Central Bank Announcements:

- Interest rate decisions and monetary policy changes

2. Economic Data Releases:

- GDP, inflation, unemployment, and more

3. Geopolitical Events:

- Elections, conflicts, and political changes

4. Natural Disasters:

- Earthquakes, hurricanes, and other crises


Trading on News Events:

1. Event-Driven Strategies:

- Trading based on expected market reactions

2. News-Based Market Analysis:

- Interpreting news impact on market trends

3. Sentiment Analysis:

- Gauging market mood and positioning


*Mastering Market News*

1. Stay Informed:

- Follow reliable news sources and market calendars

2. Analyze and Interpret:

- Understand news impact on market trends

3. Adjust Trading Strategies:

- Respond to changing market conditions

*Fundamental Analysis and Trading Decisions*

Integrating Fundamental Analysis

1. Combining with Technical Analysis:

- Balancing technical and fundamental perspectives

2. Identifying Market Trends:

- Recognizing long-term fundamental trends

3. Setting Trading Goals:

- Establishing realistic goals based on fundamental analysis

Fundamental Analysis Checklist

1. Economic Indicators:

- Assessing GDP, inflation, and employment

2. Central Bank Actions:

- Evaluating interest rate decisions and monetary policy

3. Government Policies:

- Considering fiscal policy, trade agreements, and political events

Making Informed Trading Decisions

1. Weighing Fundamental Factors:

- Assessing the impact of fundamental analysis on trading decisions

2. Adjusting for Market Sentiment:

- Considering market mood and positioning

3. Staying Adaptable:

- Responding to changing fundamental conditions

By integrating fundamental analysis into your trading approach, you can:

- Enhance trading decisions

- Identify long-term market trends

# Chapter 11: Trading Strategies and Techniques

*Overview of Trading Strategies*

Trading strategies: planned approaches to buying and selling currencies

*Common Trading Strategies*

1. Day Trading:

- Closing positions within a trading day

2. Swing Trading:

- Holding positions for a shorter term (days or weeks)

3. Position Trading:

- Holding positions for a longer term (months or years)

4. Scalping:

- Making multiple small trades in a short period

*Types of Trading Techniques*

1. Trend Following:

- Identifying and following market trends

2. Range Trading:

- Buying and selling within a specific price range

3. Breakout Trading:

- Trading on price movements outside established ranges

4. Mean Reversion:

- Identifying overbought/oversold conditions and trading on reversals

Understanding trading strategies and techniques helps traders:

- Develop a personalized trading approach

- Improve trading performance

- Manage risk effectively

*Trend Following and Range Trading*

Trend Following Strategies

1. Moving Average Crossover:

- Using MA lines to identify trend changes

2. Momentum Trading:

- Identifying strong price movements

3. Breakout Trading:

- Trading on price movements outside established trends


Range Trading Strategies

1. Support and Resistance:

- Identifying key price levels

2. Bollinger Bands:

- Using volatility-based indicators

3. Mean Reversion:

- Identifying overbought/oversold conditions


Tips for Trend Followers

1. Identify Strong Trends:

- Use indicators and chart analysis

2. Set Realistic Goals:

- Balance risk and reward

3. Stay Disciplined:

- Avoid impulsive decisions

Tips for Range Traders

1. Identify Clear Ranges:

- Use chart analysis and indicators

2. Set Tight Stops:

- Manage risk effectively

3. Monitor Market Conditions:

- Adjust strategies as needed


By mastering trend following and range trading, traders can:

- Develop effective trading strategies

- Improve market understanding

- Enhance trading performance


*Breakout Trading and Mean Reversion*

Breakout Trading Strategies:

1. Identifying Breakout Points:

- Using chart patterns and indicators

2. Setting Stop-Losses:

- Managing risk effectively

3. Scaling Positions:

- Adjusting position size based on market conditions


Mean Reversion Strategies:

1. Identifying Overbought/Oversold Conditions:

- Using indicators like RSI and Bollinger Bands

2. Setting Reversion Targets:

- Estimating price return to mean

3. Timing Entries:

- Using indicators and chart analysis

*Tips for Breakout Traders*

1. Filter Out False Breakouts:

- Using confirmation indicators

2. Stay Disciplined:

- Avoid impulsive decisions

3. Monitor Market Conditions:

- Adjust strategies as needed


*Tips for Mean Reversion Traders*

1. Identify Strong Trends:

- Use indicators and chart analysis

2. Set Realistic Targets:

- Balance risk and reward

3. Stay Patient:

- Wait for optimal entry points


By mastering breakout trading and mean reversion, traders can:

- Develop effective trading strategies

- Improve market understanding

- Enhance trading performance


*Advanced Trading Techniques*

Scalping Strategies:

1. Identifying High-Liquidity Pairs:

- Using volume and volatility indicators

2. Setting Tight Stops:

- Managing risk effectively

3. Scaling Positions:

- Adjusting position size based on market conditions

Position Trading Strategies

1. Identifying Long-Term Trends:

- Using chart analysis and indicators

2. Setting Realistic Goals:

- Balancing risk and reward

3. Staying Disciplined:

- Avoiding impulsive decisions

Carry Trading Strategies

1. Identifying Interest Rate Differentials:

- Using economic indicators and news

2. Managing Risk:

- Hedging and diversifying positions

3. Monitoring Market Conditions:

- Adjusting strategies as needed

By mastering advanced trading techniques, traders can:

- Develop sophisticated trading strategies

- Improve market understanding

- Enhance trading performance

# Chapter 12: Managing Emotions and Psychology

*Emotions in Trading*

1. Fear:

- Leading to impulsive decisions and risk aversion

2. Greed:

- Leading to overconfidence and excessive risk-taking

3. Hope:

- Leading to holding onto losing positions

4. Regret:

- Leading to revenge trading and poor decision-making


*The Importance of Emotional Control*

1. Disciplined Decision-Making:

- Separating emotions from trading decisions

2. Risk Management:

- Managing emotions to maintain a risk management strategy

3. Consistency:

- Developing a consistent trading approach


*Understanding Your Trading Personality*

1. Self-Awareness:

- Recognizing your emotional strengths and weaknesses

2. Personality Traits:

- Identifying traits that impact trading performance

3. Emotional Intelligence:

- Developing skills to manage emotions effectively

*Managing Emotions and Biases*

Common Biases in Trading:

1. Confirmation Bias:

- Seeking information that confirms your views

2. Anchoring Bias:

- Relying too heavily on initial information

3. Loss Aversion:

- Fear of losses leading to impulsive decisions

4. Overconfidence:

- Excessive faith in your trading abilities

*Strategies for Managing Emotions*

1. Mindfulness:

- Practicing self-awareness and presence

2. Journaling:

- Recording thoughts and emotions to identify patterns

3. Breathing Techniques:

- Managing stress and anxiety

4. Physical Exercise:

- Reducing stress and improving focus

*Techniques for Overcoming Biases*

1. Diversification:

- Spreading risk to minimize bias impact

2. Data-Driven Decision-Making:

- Relying on objective data

3. Seeking Diverse Perspectives:

- Encouraging alternative viewpoints

4. Regular Self-Reflection:

- Identifying and addressing biases

By managing emotions and biases, traders can:

- Improve trading performance

- Enhance decision-making

- Develop a more disciplined approach

*Building Mental Toughness*

Developing Resilience:

1. Embracing Failure:

- Learning from mistakes and setbacks

2. Practicing Self-Compassion:

- Treating yourself with kindness and understanding

3. Focusing on Progress:

- Celebrating small wins and advancements

Cultivating Confidence:

1. Setting Realistic Goals:

- Achieving milestones and building momentum

2. Developing a Growth Mindset:

- Embracing challenges and continuous learning

3. Visualizing Success:

- Imagining positive outcomes and scenarios

Managing Stress and Pressure:

1. Prioritizing Self-Care:

- Maintaining physical and mental well-being

2. Building a Support Network:

- Surrounding yourself with positive influences

3. Staying Present:

- Focusing on the current moment and task

By building mental toughness, traders can:

- Develop a stronger mindset

- Improve performance under pressure

- Enhance overall well-being

*Maintaining a Healthy Trading Mindset*

Avoiding Burnout:

1. Setting Boundaries:

- Establishing a healthy work-life balance

2. Taking Breaks:

- Regularly stepping away from trading

3. Prioritizing Relaxation:

- Engaging in stress-reducing activities

Cultivating a Positive Mindset:

1. Practicing Gratitude:

- Focusing on the positive aspects of trading

2. Reframing Negative Thoughts:

- Challenging and replacing unhelpful beliefs

3. Visualizing Success:

- Imagining positive outcomes and scenarios

Continuously Improving:

1. Seeking Feedback:

- Embracing constructive criticism and insights

2. Learning from Mistakes:

- Analyzing and growing from errors

3. Staying Adaptable:

- Embracing change and adjusting strategies

By maintaining a healthy trading mindset, traders can:

- Enhance overall well-being

- Improve trading performance

- Develop a resilient and adaptable approach

# Chapter 13: Building a Trading Plan

Defining Your Trading Objectives

1. Specific Goals:

- Clearly defining what you want to achieve

2. Measurable Outcomes:

- Quantifying success and progress

3. Realistic Expectations:

- Setting achievable targets

4. Time-Bound Objectives:

- Establishing deadlines and milestones


*Assessing Your Trading Style*

1. Risk Tolerance:

- Understanding your comfort level with risk

2. Market Analysis:

- Identifying your approach to market analysis

3. Trading Strategies:

- Determining your preferred trading methods

4. Time Commitment:

- Establishing the time you can dedicate to trading


By defining your trading objectives and assessing your trading style, you can:

- Create a tailored trading plan

- Increase your chances of success

- Develop a clear direction for your trading journey

*Developing a Trading Strategy*

1. Defining Your Edge:

- Identifying what sets you apart from other traders

2. Market Analysis:

- Determining your approach to market analysis (technical, fundamental, or sentiment-based)

3. Trade Selection:

- Establishing criteria for entering and exiting trades

4. Risk Management:

- Defining risk-reward ratios and position sizing

*Common Trading Strategies*

1. Trend Following:

- Identifying and riding market trends

2. Range Trading:

- Buying and selling within established price ranges

3. Mean Reversion:

- Identifying overbought/oversold conditions and betting on a return to mean

4. Breakout Trading:

- Entering trades when prices break through established levels

By developing a trading strategy, you can:

- Increase consistency and discipline

- Improve trading performance

- Enhance confidence and decision-making

*Creating a Trading Plan Framework*

I. Market Analysis

1. Market Conditions:

  - Identifying market trends, sentiment, and volatility

  2. Instrument Analysis:

  - Selecting specific markets or instruments to trade

II. Trade Entry and Exit

  1. Entry Criteria:

  - Defining conditions for entering trades

  2. Exit Criteria:

  - Establishing rules for exiting trades

III. Risk Management

  1. Position Sizing:

  - Determining optimal position size

  2. Stop-Losses:

  - Setting stop-loss levels to limit losses

  3. Take-Profit:

  - Establishing take-profit levels to secure gains

IV. Performance Monitoring

  1. Trade Tracking:

  - Recording and analyzing trade performance

  2. Performance Metrics:

  - Establishing key performance indicators (KPIs)


By creating a trading plan framework, you can:

- Develop a clear and structured approach to trading

- Improve discipline and consistency

- Enhance overall trading performance

*Implementing and Refining Your Trading Plan*

Implementation:

1. Start Small:

- Begin with a limited scope and gradually expand

2. Monitor Progress:

- Track performance and adjust as needed

3. Stay Disciplined:

- Adhere to your plan, avoiding impulsive decisions


Refining Your Plan:

1. Regular Review:

- Schedule regular reviews to assess performance

2. Analyze Mistakes:

- Identify areas for improvement and adjust strategies

3. Stay Adaptable:

- Be willing to adjust your plan as market conditions change


*Common Pitfalls to Avoid*

1. Over-Optimization:

- Avoid over-analyzing and tweaking your plan excessively

2. Lack of Discipline:

- Stay committed to your plan, avoiding impulsive decisions

3. Failure to Adapt:

- Be willing to adjust your plan as market conditions evolve

By implementing and refining your trading plan, you can:

- Develop a robust and effective trading approach

- Improve trading performance and consistency

- Enhance your overall trading journey

# Chapter 14: Advanced Forex Concepts

*Forex Market Dynamics*

Understanding Market Structure

1. Market Participants:

- Identifying key players (banks, institutions, retail traders)

2. Order Flow:

- Analyzing the flow of buy and sell orders

3. Liquidity:

- Understanding the availability of trades at various price levels


Market Sentiment and Psychology

1. Bullish and Bearish Sentiment:

- Identifying market attitudes and trends

2. Market Emotions:

- Understanding how emotions drive trading decisions

3. Crowd Psychology:

- Analyzing how market participants influence each other


*Advanced Charting Techniques*

1. Multi-Time Frame Analysis:

- Analyzing charts across different time frames

2. Chart Patterns:

- Identifying complex patterns and formations

3. Technical Indicators:

- Using advanced indicators to inform trading decisions

By understanding advanced forex concepts, you can:

- Develop a deeper understanding of market dynamics

- Improve trading performance and decision-making

- Enhance your overall market analysis skills

*Advanced Technical Analysis*

Trend Analysis:

1. Higher Highs and Higher Lows:

- Identifying uptrends

2. Lower Highs and Lower Lows:

- Identifying downtrends

3. Trend Lines:

- Drawing lines to connect highs and lows

Chart Patterns:

1. Triangles:

- Identifying symmetrical, ascending, and descending triangles

2. Wedges:

- Identifying rising and falling wedges

3. Head and Shoulders:

- Identifying reversals and continuations

Candlestick Patterns:

1. Reversal Patterns:

- Identifying hammer, shooting star, and engulfing patterns

2. Continuation Patterns:

- Identifying three white soldiers and three black crows

3. Indecision Patterns:

- Identifying doji and spinning top patterns

By mastering advanced technical analysis, you can:

- Improve your ability to identify trends and patterns

- Enhance your trading decisions with precise timing

- Develop a more nuanced understanding of market dynamics

*Advanced Forex Concepts*

Risk Management Strategies

1. Position Sizing:

- Calculating optimal position size based on risk tolerance

2. Stop-Loss Strategies:

- Using static, trailing, and dynamic stop-losses

3. Hedging and Diversification:

- Reducing risk through hedging and diversifying trades

Advanced Trading Techniques

1. Scalping:

- Taking advantage of small price movements

2. Day Trading:

- Closing trades within a single trading day

3. Swing Trading:

- Holding trades for several days or weeks

Forex Trading Psychology

1. Emotional Control:

- Managing fear, greed, and emotional decision-making

2. Discipline and Patience:

- Sticking to trading plans and waiting for opportunities

3. Adaptability:

- Adjusting to changing market conditions and trends

By mastering advanced forex concepts, you can:

- Develop a sophisticated trading approach

- Improve risk management and trading performance

- Enhance your overall trading psychology and discipline

*Forex Trading Automation*

1. Expert Advisors (EAs):

- Using automated trading software for MetaTrader

2. Algorithmic Trading:

- Developing and implementing automated trading strategies

3. Trade Copying and Mirroring:

- Copying trades from experienced traders or signal providers

*Forex Market Analysis Tools*

1. Economic Indicators:

- Analyzing GDP, inflation, and employment data

2. Sentiment Analysis:

- Gauging market sentiment through news and social media

3. Market Correlations:

- Identifying relationships between currency pairs and markets

*Advanced Forex Trading Strategies*

1. Carry Trading:

- Profiting from interest rate differentials

2. Range Trading:

- Buying and selling within established price ranges

3. Breakout Trading:

- Identifying and capitalizing on price breakouts

By understanding advanced forex concepts, you can:

- Develop a comprehensive trading approach

- Improve trading performance and consistency

- Enhance your overall market analysis and trading skills

# Chapter 15: Conclusion and Final Thoughts

*Summary of Key Takeaways*

Congratulations on completing this comprehensive guide to forex trading! Let's recap some key takeaways:

1. Forex Market Fundamentals:

- Understanding the forex market structure and participants

2. Trading Strategies and Techniques:

- Mastering various trading approaches and methods

3. Risk Management and Psychology:

- Developing a disciplined and informed trading mindset

4. Advanced Forex Concepts:

- Exploring sophisticated trading strategies and tools


Remember:

- Forex trading carries risks and requires continuous learning

- Discipline, patience, and adaptability are essential for success

- Stay informed, but avoid emotional decision-making


Final Thoughts

- Forex trading is a journey, not a destination

- Continuous improvement and learning are crucial

- Stay curious, and always be open to new ideas and strategies

- Remember, success in forex trading takes time, effort, and perseverance

- Stay focused, and don't be afraid to ask for help

Next Steps:

1. Practice and Refine Your Skills:

- Continue practicing and refining your trading strategies

2. Stay Informed and Up-to-Date:

- Stay current with market news, analysis, and trends

3. Join a Trading Community:

- Connect with other traders to share knowledge and experiences

4. Set Realistic Goals and Track Progress:

- Set achievable goals and track your progress regularly


Additional Resources:

- Recommended reading and online resources for further learning

- Forex trading communities and forums for connecting with other traders

By following these next steps and staying committed to your trading journey, you'll be well on your way to achieving success in the forex markets.

This concludes the comprehensive guide to forex trading. I hope you found it informative and helpful. Happy trading!